A PALACE OF RUINS

A PALACE OF RUINS

Poems

Steve Nolan

RAGGED SKY PRESS  *Princeton, New Jersey*

Copyright © 2023 by Steve Nolan

Published by Ragged Sky Press

270 Griggs Drive

Princeton, NJ 08540

raggedsky.com

All Rights Reserved

ISBN 978-1-93397455-2

Library of Congress Control Number: 2023941412

Cover photo: War art on buildings in Irpin, Ukraine, courtesy of
Edward Matthews/Alamy Stock Photo

Text and cover design: Pamela L. Schnitter

This book has been composed in Verdigris MVB and Profile

Printed on acid-free paper. ∞

Printed in the United States of America

CONTENTS

III

I

The more we are awake the more we are participating
in the awakening of humanity.

—HAZRAT INAYAT KHAN

STUDENT BODY

(for Dr. Christopher Bursk, 1943–2021)

He seemed embarrassed by his body
as if some god had given him
the wrong size suit to wear
to work, to church, in public. Yet
he made it lumber, stumble, stoop,
ever-leaning forward, not a planet
locked into an orbit, but a meteor.

He taught others to embrace
their own bodies, their own bodily
functions, their own desires, mistakes
and accidents. Learning
a way to overcome imperfection,
shame, whether a freshman matriculating
from incestuous abuse, or an inmate
writing a poem about hands
put in a cell because of crimes
he hardly believes they committed.

He collected students like a philatelist,
preserving stamps, each put on a page,
given a name for rarity, the unusual
more valuable—never the freak show
they thought they brought to him—
everyone a phase of the moon,
a sliver of hope, a harvest, the teacher
himself reflected light in night sky
that some other poet said, comes,
like answered prayers, once a blue moon.

THE LAUREATE'S LOVE POEMS

(for Carly)

She said she didn't know how to write a love poem,
lacked the pedigree to be a subject-
matter expert. She read poetry of pain
(a little girl under a bridge,
a teenage encounter with a pervert),
the stories children tell themselves to feel safe,
the ciphering necessary for sanity,
the way we find hallowed ground
in the ordinary—every audience member
reminded of their own journey, each
discovery of the sacred, a love poem
in progress. Revision essential, editing required.

Anne Frank did not know how to write
a love poem. At thirteen she lacked
the knowledge of romantic love; but nothing's
more romantic than the ordeal—the journey
down the birth canal toward light,
hiding oneself behind a bookcase
that might contain a Bible or *Mein Kampf*.
Nothing's more romantic than a girl's longing
for what she dreams into existence.

An infant's first breath brings a cry,
the first word of a love poem,
the only love poem ever written.

POETS AS BUTTERFLIES

We crawl out of Covid, each-their-own
way, masked and unmasked, depending
on vulnerability, shortening the social
distance to individual taste; dining
in public now on the rise. Tonight,
reinstitution of poetry night
at the public library—the featured poet
a laureate of a county in Pennsylvania.

Spring has arrived and we are conscious
on some level of the miracle of new life
emerging from winter, or the deeper thought
that it is not new life but the same
life resurrected, and that we are
facsimiles of Magdalene at the tomb.

The featured poet, like all poets, has something
to say about nature, how insignificant
we are to the stars, to the moon,
though they stay faithful to us, witness
our passing as they remain. Everyone

of us has some injury, some disease
festering, some souvenirs of the aging process,
physical or psychological; and the audacity
to want to share our glint of illumination.

Poets pluck common threads from the tapestry
with as much hubris but less certainty
than clergy preaching life's shoulds and shouldn'ts—

the poet marvels at the mystery
of every flower, every beetle devouring
beauty, every bee perpetuating it,
every butterfly burst from a chrysalis,
beckoning you to follow its path
with no idea of where it is going,
where it will land, what warm breezes
will carry it, and no worries about
the many winters to come, simply the rapture,
the fluttering experience of being alive.

NAMING FIREFLIES

They appear and disappear like a meteor shower
resurrected to new life after burning out.
We spread our blanket, unpack a picnic

lunch as the sun sets on Tanglewood's
evening concert series. Tonight: J. S. Bach,
who could hear the music of the spheres,

inspiring concertos, consecrating mass.
I don't know how many patrons share
Bach's faith, but all see these pulsations

of light in the darkening air. Too dark now
to see their bodies, but with concentration
it is possible to follow the flight path

of a single lightning bug. I make
a game of this, foiled when they cross
paths with another. I remember

trapping them in jars, martyring them
to posses their light, showing off
for other kids. The envelope of night

descends. Bach suddenly joins the light
parade and I question if I've drunk too much
wine because I swear they're blinking in sync

with the Musica Universalis—
celestial bodies: sun, moon, planets,
lightning bugs in orbit. My wife takes

my hand and I wonder if she's thinking of Yemen
or Syria, the peace and reconciliation work
she did in Rwanda? If she squeezes

hard I know she will make me cry.
There are many light workers in the world,
so much darkness I am staring into—

straining not to lose sight of Jesus,
Buddha, Gandhi—it is the wine!
I am naming fireflies.

MERELY A DOG PASSING

(for Annie)

No peace on earth,
no battles won,
no laws passed,
no charitable donations given,
no measurable accomplishments of any kind;
simply time shared through
thousands of custodial duties
performed out of necessity
more than kindness,
what humans might call friendship.
           We did walk the same streets,
bask by the same hearth,
sit together for countless hours
in the same back yard
for so many seasons,
me reading—her sleeping
through milestone
moments of my life
with friends and family.
           She would wait patiently
registering no jealousy
at my enthusiasm for time spent
away from her earning money, paying bills,
talking with children and grandchildren.
She joined the furniture, kitchen pots and pans,
morning paper delivery—
every less-than-relevant window dressing
we assemble to adorn our lives—
the fixtures that give comfort
by their known proximity.

Then she was gone,
merely a dog passing—
much more than any shooting star
on a summer night
that we take the time to follow
but never the time to ponder
where did that come from
and why was that brief flare
so satisfying.

SLAVE DIARY

(the slave who wrote in Arabic)

My name is Omar Ibn Said.
My birthplace is Fut Tur (Senegal).
My parents encouraged my studies—
for twenty-five years: the Koran,
philosophy, theology, astronomy.
There came to my country a big army.
Many people were killed. They took me
and walked me to the sea, sold me
to a Christian man who walked me
to a big ship. We sailed the big sea
for a month and a half until we came
to a place called Charleston. I was sold
to an evil man who did not fear Allah
at all. *All praise to the most merciful,
the compassionate.* Slaves are to be
delivered from bondage. The good book
says the seas were parted for God's chosen.
The seas did not part for me, a pagan
from homicidal Africa; so said
the infidel. He has a prayer that says
deliver us from evil and give us this day
our daily bread—meted out by those
whom God allows to exercise their will
freely, as freely as Iblis,
the one the Christian calls Satan.

AMONG THE BLESSED

*(following an exhibition by the artist
and poet Patricia Goodrich)*

We witness a man suffocated by another man's knee,
an Old Testament act awakening an un-woke nation
out of a grey faith. The artist picks up shards
of blue glass from the broken window of a synagogue
in Budapest and pockets them.

We find relics. We put them in boxes,
we turn them into altars, we collect
candles and holy water, we pray
before crucifixes or treasure a piece
of the Berlin Wall—anything that can stir
hope for salvation or the comfort
of feeling small under a great Western
sky hiding a divinity on the outside
looking in over the Land of Enchantment
with its poetry, flies, and bones.

Some things need to stay open:
the echo chamber of human memory
that collects what's been discarded—
an accordion, perhaps a polka,
the random feather of a songbird.

GIVE US THIS DAY

Each day he brings fresh fruit and rice,
places it on his homemade altar,
an offering for the dead, with no claim
that any portion disappears or is partially
eaten like cookies left for Santa.
To nonbelievers he is the mindless fool
repeating superstition, a relic of centuries
past, where daily life was blessed or cursed
by friendly and unfriendly ghosts. His grand-
children talk to him with a loving condescension
about his departed wife, their grandmother,
for whom they've never lit a candle, invited
with incense or prayer. They stay distracted
by frequent messages from another ether,
registering in their earbuds. They smile
and whisper about waste as he removes
the shriveled fruit, the hardened rice and shuffles
to the garden to feed the birds, fill
the bath. He watches the bird's ablutions,
imagining the delight his wife derived
from these visitations, this zest,
this appetite, this communion,
this offering: the most we get to give
the living or the dead.

LABYRINTH

(Kripalu Yoga Center)

The plaque suggests I enter as if walking
into sacred space, so I recite
the prayers from my childhood,
the ones taught by those guiding
my steps upon a righteous path.
> I pause at the entrance, set an intention
> and I wonder if my mother set
> an intention as she birthed me.
It says *walk mindfully at whatever pace
I want.* Once in the center, it says,
stop to notice the views, smells, sounds
and I think of midlife, the crisis that comes
from how long you've ignored those cues.
> Finally—*walk out following the path
> you walked in on*—I walked
> in with cancer, cause unknown, possibly
> from following too many instructions.
I stare at the Buddha
and Saint Francis statues—
people who learned to follow
their own footsteps. I cut across
the labyrinth paths, over
the mowed fields, down
to the lake. A chipmunk scurries
for safety in the underbrush,
geese crowd the shoreline,
some gliding gracefully, others
fishing for something below the surface,
serenely confident in their purpose,

no roads, no prayers, no labyrinth
to tread to find their center, no
guru to tell them who they are.

OUR FIRST ARGUMENT AFTER YOUR DEATH

(for NJ)

I suppose it would be more accurate
to call it disagreement; argument requires
give and take and I can hear you saying,
"I'm dead, stupid, you're talking to yourself."
That was the major difference between us—
disbelief insisting on its own extinction,
belief conjuring up a prayer, the subject
of a prayer, the way the painter tries to turn
shadow and light into something permanent.
Renaissance masters, passed on their optics
as a gift to the neophyte. Load up your palette,
empty it onto canvas so finite
a museum fire seemingly erases history.

You believed in ashes-to-ashes philosophy
so as not to be sentimental or superstitious.
I believe in the little girl crying
at the loss of irreplaceable relics;
who became an artist, so that beauty wouldn't
die—but transition—into sun and soil,
wind that I shout into, listening for your voice
talking back to me—even if it is saying,
"You are imagining things."

AFTER A DAY IN STRASBOURG

Timothe led me to the cemetery,
an unlikely stop biking
with a five-year-old, until
I realized it was just curiosity,
his breather in the shade from the dusty farm
road, a hilltop setting, if you could
call it a hilltop, more like a rise
in elevation; but still a fitting burial
place for soldiers always looking for
some advantage in war. The names were German,
and only eight headstones to memorialize
them in the French countryside, along
with a large Iron Cross set in a cairn,
and a few stone steps, perfect for
a five-year-old boy to climb while escorting
an American soldier, now a grandfather,
who spoke no French and the boy no English,
his parents my hosts, his father my wife's
foreign-exchange student from many years
before. Timothe tapped the stones with a stick,
reciting something that sounded like a nursery
rhyme, while I sounded the names:
Hallman, Von Petersdorf, Podschalowski,
Von Devitz, Von Sack…
And then a silent nod for the unknown…
tried to say them with honor as if
they weren't an enemy, some rabble bent
on conquest or war crimes, but just boys
like Timothe, swashbucklers, Jack
Sparrows, with cutlasses, eye-patches,
hooks, peg-legs, all manner of prosthetics,

and a parrot on the shoulder of the captain
mimicking whatever it's been taught: "Polly
want a cracker" made of German or French
wheat, which in Alsace would depend on
the decade; the mothers, of children like Timothe,
told what flag their sons would die for.
And in between wars those boys off
to university drinking beer made
with the same wheat, trying to keep pace
with a girl on a bike with a baguette, who might
make them wait a year for a kiss,
but just might be their future wife.
Timothe led me back to our trusted mounts,
back through the fields on the rutted road,
we pedalled toward a darkening sky—
the wheat, the corn, the small boy,
dependent on storm clouds rising.

AN ASSAULT ON TRUTH

A young girl named Anne has to hide
in an attic, a young boy in Africa is asked,
"What do you want to be when you grow up?"
And he says, "Alive." Audrey Hepburn
asked that question as a UNICEF ambassador.
She was the same age as Anne Frank
under Nazi occupation in the Netherlands.
She would say for the rest of her life,
"That was the girl who didn't make it,
and I did." She was not into
building walls, not into calling
Nazis "fine people," a firm believer
in doing for the least of our brethren,
preferred an affordable wardrobe, flats
to stilettos, did not eat breakfast
at Tiffany's in real life, but helped
bring food to the Sudan and Ethiopia.
I had a crush on her as a boy, a woman
old enough to be my mother;

my mother, who also opposed Nazis,
helped liberate camps, medically treat
the survivors. I took her to Utah Beach,
where she landed in Normandy. Sixty years
later, we walked the strand. It was low
tide, on her face a flood of memory.
We climbed to the high ground, crawled into
the German bunkers, briefly slipped into
the uniform of the enemy, felt
the profound quiet and peace of the place—
grateful that love is more powerful

than hate, gazed out over Omaha,
the receding channel. I was contemplating
history, wondering what she was thinking—
she and my father caught in war, her two
older sons surviving Vietnam,
her baby boy yet to go to Afghanistan.
We stood together in silence, knowing we must
live with lunatics and lunar cycles,
knowing the tide must come back again.

EMPTY NEST

"I'm scared, don't go," my mother said
to my sister, who had just cleaned up
the mess. It was official now—my mother
was incontinent. My sister had finally won
the long struggle, broken through, convinced
her to wear *Depends*. After the shower,
the fresh PJ's, the shitty sheets stripped
and fresh linen spread on the bed, she
seemed ready to be tucked in—but she
was suddenly upset, confused, "Where
is everybody?"
              "Your children?" my sister asked,
and my mother nodded. Then the explanation—
four residing out of state, a son
living across town. "I wish they were here,"
she said in her ninety-eight-year-old voice
which had lost them all to time—the one thing
even love loses its grip on.

WHERE IS JESUS?

A friend told me his church removes
the crucified Christ from the cross
on Good Friday. The first time this happened
he asked his priest, "Where's Jesus?"
and he was shown the basement storage room
where Jesus reclined amongst the terra cotta
garden pots, the roach motels, and rat
poison canisters—my friend said Jesus
looked just as peaceful and tortured there,
but abandoned.
          When I was a boy
I saw Michelangelo's *Pieta*
at the New York World's Fair.
We came from the suburbs in a big
blue Buick station wagon. I knew
nothing of children living with cockroaches
or rats in the basements of any New York
tenement, although I did have to eat
all my food because of starving children
in Calcutta.
          Jesus lay on his back
staring at the ceiling while people squeezed
into pews, dressed to the nines, waiting
for him to resurrect from the storage room.

The Apostle's Creed says, ...*he suffered under
Pontius Pilate, was crucified, died
and was buried; he descended into hell.
On the third day he rose from the dead.*

I always forget that he descended into hell
before his ascent to heaven to be seated
at the hand of the Father Almighty.

> "Where's Jesus?" my friend said.
> "I'll show you," said the holy man.

PEACE BE UPON YOU

(for Tony in Syria in gratitude for his echoes from the heart)

There is so much corruption here—
desperate people in every camp.
When this nightmare is over I will
take my boy and girl to Canada
if there is no more room at the Inn.

I have adopted two children.
My son: running out of the tent,
"I'm not playing Chinese Checkers with her
anymore, because she's cheating."
Me: "Are you cheating in there?"
My daughter: "No sir! I'm in here helping
myself win, but I'm surely not cheating!"

I have grown a beard to keep my face warm.
My memories of heat, of Desert Storm,
they come and go. They brought me glad tidings—
the new president returned support to our
Kurdish allies who had been betrayed.
Com-passion means to *suffer with*.

I have night watch tonight.
Jaddah, our adopted grandmother,
brought me *barazek*—warm cookies
with butter, sweet honey, and vanilla,
roasted sesame seeds on one side,
roasted pistachios on the other.

This is what saves the human race.
There is no such thing as an ordinary human being.

WONDERFUL WORLD

(Satchmo)

Louis Armstrong could see a sunrise over a mountain.
He could not choose his own water fountain
but could see how people like to feed pigeons
in outdoor cafes;
                        segregated buses,
segregated restaurants, segregated
hotels, Jim Crow the law even
for returning war heroes—God
troubling the waters everywhere
but there was always a shepherd, always a fisherman
from his view, reaching out a hand saying
"How do you do?" And deep-down knowing,
that they were really saying, "I love you."
He heard babies crying, smelled roses
too, joined bees singing under
a sky of blue—all the colors of the rainbow
in the people that he knew;
                            lugged his trumpet
and sweaty handkerchief home after a long
smoky night, looked up at the starry heavens
after breaking up a fight, and said
to himself, "What a wonderful world."

THE REAL REASON I CALL HER MY BETTER HALF

It seemed to complete some season,
to bring some purpose to my life in the garden—
beyond walking around every day naming things
for no one—not even myself,
with my unpracticed memory.

Paradise was a piece of mango—
all the fruit low hanging. I now know
that it was the knowledge of good and evil
for which I needed a helpmate.

I see why that's the forbidden fruit,
how it can bring pain and suffering,
how the virgin's life could be a type of Paradise—
where the lion lies down with the lamb
in a Peaceable Kingdom
like a never-ending pleasant dream
where everything is safe but nothing is interesting.

We made our choice and we can pretend
for others that it was not Divinely Planned
by the All-Knowing One. But, I tell you now,
I never really trusted the architect of Paradise
and this lower earth until you whispered,
"Open your eyes" and I discovered
the Image and Likeness had a heart

and we consecrated our love
not just with blood
but with tears.

II

Your job is to find out what the world is trying to be.
—WILLIAM STAFFORD

STATESIDE (PTS WITHOUT THE D)

My wife said when I got home from Afghanistan that I once punched a gas pump out of frustration, because it wouldn't take my credit card; my oldest daughter says that I had some anger problems for about six months. I don't have the energy to try to argue with their memories or perception just because it does not match mine.

I do remember a barbeque where I was not interested in any of the guests. I remember relishing my role as master of the grill because it gave me an excuse to be separate, to nurse a beer or two in solitary confinement. Nonetheless, I could still hear their conversations about buying a new cell phone or the chances of our local football team winning the championship.

I preferred to think about a soldier who had been shot through the thigh, the bullet shattering his femur, severing his femoral artery. I was anxious to receive a phone call from a chaplain buddy of mine who promised to tell me if the soldier kept his leg. I looked around the 4th of July celebration, happy to be home, sure now that others noticed my silence, how I preferred to keep to myself, how they would conclude that the war had changed me, not the same person who left, not quite right in the head; certain that I was the only sane person at the party.

WHITE GLOVES

(Bereavement counseling in my official capacity for the
U.S. government)

Dorothy let me in
because I'd seen Afghanistan,
roamed the same territory
that killed her son—a roadside bomb
negating all his combat skills.
She offered coffee, pastry she'd made
for my visit. I accepted—God help anyone who wouldn't.
I don't remember the confection but I
remember childhood pictures, the smiling
second baseman, the high school football star,
and finally, the estranged daughter-in-law,
the grandson she swore was an identical
twin; her hands wanting, needing to hold
more than the picture. She said she'd heard
from the soldier who was wounded in
the same blast, had talked with his mother,
that it helped—as had meeting
the vice president and his wife at the Gold
Star family gathering in Washington;
how they showed sincerity and kindness.

She wanted me to know about Dover,
how the whole base stopped work
the moment her son's plane touched down;
how they handled the casket with dignity,
how the white gloves moved in slow motion,
ushered him sacramentally on his way
to his resting place, how clean those hands,
how careful not to jostle the traveler,

how bright against their combat uniforms,
against the flag that draped the casket.

And when they slid their brother into the hearse:
the white gloves, empty of duty, paused
for one frozen second, like doves of peace
almost ready for flight.

ENEMY OF THE PEOPLE

The first thing they did to Jamal Khashoggi
in the Saudi Consulate in Istanbul,
was cut off his fingers
for making love to the written word.
Eventually they cut off his head,
which contains the tongue.

The leader of the free world sent
a clear message that he did not want
to jeopardize business deals
for one individual life; and took
the time to educate: at least five
other arms dealers could fill the void…

…Do not let this man visit a kindergarten,
do not let this man take your scouts
into the forest. Do not let your daughters
drink with him at a frat party.

I will leave the Dodge Poetry Festival,
Newark, New Jersey, take the train home,
sit down and type this poem
with fingers still able to move freely.
Ten little "enemies of the people."

POSTMORTEM HOUSE CLEANING

(6 March 19)

My niece and I pore through the photo albums,
boxes of loose, curled, snapshots never
categorized, framed, mounted on a wall.
She finds a handful of images of the massacre
at Gardelegen—there is a barn door
opened by American soldiers, bodies
one on top of another at the entrance.

Four feet to the left of the pile is the face
of a young man who managed to dig a hole
from the inside, get his head into the open air.
His shoulder blades never made it; the rest
of his body suffered the intended fate—all burned
alive in the barricaded barn under
the direction of the SS before they fled—
the fire meant to destroy evidence (and evidence
it is), kept in a box by a 98-year-old woman
with a plethora of war photos mostly documenting
medical personnel doing their duty, doing
their damn best to save every life possible.

I take out my cellphone, click a picture
of the picture, send it to several friends,
proud of my mother's involvement, wanting to send
a message of "Never again!" since the leader
of the free world just declared himself
a nationalist, said from the bottom of his heart
that there were fine people on both sides.

SUNFLOWERS

This dawn holds less promise than ever before,
the trees black bones against sky,
the orange and pink of gladness trying to awaken
out of a frigid night…so many refugees
on train platforms, crowded in subways,
sitting in cars at a border crossing,
petrol dwindling, children crying, women
adjusting hoods, mittens, diapers or
tending to a dog that could not be abandoned.

Over five million displaced civilians
deliberate targets, sons, brothers, husbands,
even grandfathers taking up arms
rather than accept pending slavery—
their young president refusing safe passage,
telling the world truth is Ukraine's greatest
weapon against military superiority—
cruise missiles, cluster bombs, vacuum
blasts designed to burn and suffocate.

And the little man with the button, the mad genius,
like his American stable-mate, promising
fire and fury the likes of which the world
has never seen, rises this same morning
with no thought of the mystery and bounty
of mother earth, but rather the pleasure felt,
when the hand of the star grabs what it wants.

A mother rocks her baby and sings softly
in the quickening morning light, her thought:

what gives one man the right
to decide who gets to see another sun—
even
at Chernobyl sunflowers continue to grow.

BUCHA, UKRAINE

Stop insisting the images remain distant
for personal comfort, for the body, for
the mind to relax, to bring slumber,
for our children not to feel guilt
about impotence, for the alibi
of absence from the scene of the crime.

Bucha should be the name of every blue
bicycle a child gets to ride to the park
without negotiating smoldering tanks;
the name of nail polish used for that perfect
manicure on the one hand, of the one body,
of the one woman shot riding her bike
home from work—the decision she made
(like the founding of the United Nations)
to paint one nail with a tiny heart.

"Bucha"—say it—don't armor your heart.
Let it be a prayer—one more bead
on a rosary of sorrowful mysteries.

COMING DRY OUT OF WATER

There's a black mist over Bucha.

People in the city council told her,
"How do we know you are you?" Though
she lived her entire life in this town,
she has no passport or identity documents,
not a single piece of paper to show
who she is that was not burned in the fire
started by a hand grenade—nothing
that can get her through a military checkpoint.

She dreams of her old house: lying in bed
watching TV, her husband walking through
the door, taking off his cap, and then
his greeting, "Kitty, I'm home." Her husband was
forty years old, a welder. She was eight
years older than him. "I stole him,"
she says, of the love of her life.

She looks at the burned beams of her house,
the burned pots on the stove, somewhere
in the ash the bodies of her dog and two cats.
Her husband? His body and what was left of his head
were taken away in a body bag by a local
tattoo artist. She begged the soldier to shoot
her too. War crimes are hard to prove.
Perpetrators are hard to find. "Russians
are good at coming dry out of water," she says.

THE WORLD ECONOMIC FORUM DECIDES TO SIT SHIVA

(Ukraine exhibit, Davos, Switzerland, 2023)

A man sits on a park bench.
His face is buried in his hands.
The body of a woman lies at his feet.
Her purse sits on the bench next to him;
one of her feet is bare, one has a shoe.

A pomegranate of blood soaks through
the cloth in the middle of her chest.
Her dress is yellow.
His shirt is blue.

There is often not family for funerals
and too many dispersed to summon for Shiva.
There are no mirrors left to cover.

But Ukraine is you.

INALIENABLE

A man stood in front of a tank
with shopping bags in both hands;

a soldier begs to stay in a combat zone
despite a head wound. A journalist
covers their third war in body armor
with no weapon. The Purple Heart recipient
becomes a veteran against the war. Peter
betrayed Christ in his moment of need
so maybe no one is predictable.

Ten thousand people died in Tiananmen
Square, wounded female students
were bayonetted as they begged
for life. Pro-democracy demonstrators
were slaughtered by the 27th Group Army
of Shanxi Province—

but not the man with the shopping bags
and not the other unnamed man inside
the tank who kept stopping, and stopping,
holding up a line of armored vehicles,
putting the orders of an entire government
on hold for one conscientious objection.

SEEKING CONFIRMATION

She appeared to be an easy target.
She had been drinking

and wandered into the wrong part of the house.
He was waiting for her with an accomplice.

They were to take turns.
One stood guard,

the other muzzled her.
There was a struggle.

The look-out joined the fray.
All three fell off the bed, onto the floor.

In the alcoholic confusion
she managed to escape—

we can't find these men
because they are everywhere.

FENCES

Something there is that doesn't love a wall,
　　—ROBERT FROST

"I don't want to talk politics,"
my neighbor says, reminiscent of Frost
with his neighbor mending their wall together.
The finality of his statement like stones
not disturbed by winter cold or spring
thaw, as he lets slip a contempt for our
President greater than our enemy;
and my rebuttal merely a form of walling
in or out. He elaborates:
"My parents told me never to discuss
politics or religion." And I recognize
the cliché from my own parents, the wisdom
and the ignorance of it—the fencing so that cows
can't mingle nor apples be shared. My wife
will soon start gardening, coaxing from loam
all kinds of possibilities invisible
these long months—the miracle of seed
waiting to crack, germinate, reach for sky,
none programmed to die before blooming,
before fruiting. She does use netting
to keep rabbit and deer from the strawberries,
and she has built boxes to contain
the tomatoes; but come summer we will carry
containers of peppers, cukes and cherry toms
to this man who likes a man who likes a man
who slaughters children, who put targets on
my brothers and sisters in Afghanistan.
I will manage to stifle an anger that would
have me spew money, break the tables

of those defiling my father's and mother's house.
I will help my wife with the harvesting,
deliver radishes, offer the neighborly spinach,
see to it my seeds of rage find unfertile soil.

BROKEN EAGLE

A friend calls us the eagle and the dove,
due to my military career and my wife's
lifetime work for peace and social justice.
We both turned seventy this year,
officially becoming elders, embracing the idea
of wisdom, while experiencing the disabilities
of aging. We lost three friends this weekend,
two to cancer—shocking news that will
now be more frequent; and each time
force me into meditation as I enter
the eighth year of my own terminal illness.

Broken eagle is perhaps a better nickname
for this old soldier who has witnessed death
and destruction overseas; and now
the brokenness of my own government
by domestic enemies. "Stop the Steal"
was the rallying cry, a bloody battle
for something that did not exist.

"The truth is irrelevant" KGB Colonel
Putin once said and an American narcissist
embraced that gospel with religious zealotry.
He watched his rag-tag army of white supremacists
attack the Capitol all day long
and told those who assaulted law enforcement,
in order to break and enter a building, "We love you."

When the insurrection was over, a Congressman
took a garbage bag and started to clean
up the trash that littered the halls of Congress.

In the debris he found a broken eagle—
snapped from the masthead of an American flag.
He took it home, a souvenir of the chaos,
he showed his family. His oldest boy asked,
"What happened at work today, daddy?"

Exactly two years later Congress voted-in
a new Speaker of the House. The Speaker
accepted a phone call from and thanked the leader
of the insurrection for helping him secure
his position—it's called a quid pro quo—
you break the wing, you limit the freedom,
and the bird is yours for the taking.

It's been said, "You can leave the war but the war never leaves you." You come home and they expect you to put on a demonstration of the better angels of your nature as if you have come through rehab and recovery ready to jettison the cane, the walker, the wheelchair—just another commencement exercise, a graduation from hell stamped with a bronze star, a profile of George Washington on your heart.

I've been told Native Americans have ceremonies for the returning warrior, sweat lodges and ritual chanting that goes on for days to get the head straight. The medicine man able to awaken certain essential elements, not dull them like the bartender.

P.T Barnum could take the bruised and battered, elevate their self-esteem, yet it was also a freak show: the Siamese twins, the bearded lady, finally belonging to a tribe even if small children recoiled in horror.

The glass eye, the titanium leg, the grafted skin taken from the buttocks or thigh to reconstruct a face that won't repulse—baby steps for the things beyond repair. Little blue pills for erectile dysfunction, a whole pharmacy for emotional discord.

After Afghanistan I became a shaman for the Department of Veterans Affairs, a therapist, a snake handler, master of a three-ring-circus of clowns who wore the painted mask of the keeper of secrets: the honor of protecting and serving and the burden of living with others who cannot

understand. The ancient task of the warrior class never ends
as war never ends—each family given a new explanation for
the body bag.

Rudyard Kipling said,
"If any question why we died,
tell them because our fathers lied."

You wonder at the lies that led to Flanders, to Normandy,
the jungles of Vietnam, the deserts of Iraq—the cannons
rumbling as we speak in Kharkiv, in Mariupol; the
prolongation of madness, the survivor's grief already
started, societal post-traumatic stress, how it all begins on
the knee of the father and mother, the gospel of struggle
as old as the Bible, as new as the funerals in Israel and
Palestine.

Forty years after his war a man came to me for guidance.
The government of Vietnam was returning the remains of
his best friend to a widow who had last seen the deceased
four decades before and she asked him if he would preside
over the funeral ceremony. "How do you feel about that," I
asked, and he said he was worried, that it had taken him so
many years to put the war behind. He was afraid this might
stir it all up again. I validated his concern, it was indeed a
gamble, anxiety versus closure, but I had to ask, "Who else
can honor his sacrifice?"

He went. Of course he went.
His presence like a flag over a coffin
saying this was the place,
for a while, you called home.

THE SIXTH DAY

(based on a letter received by the Irish poet, Michael Longely)
The mother of the ice cream man
wrote the poet a letter. Her son
was murdered during *The Troubles*
in Northern Ireland. She was not
a literary person, he doubted she read
much poetry but she was moved by the fact
that someone outside the family could honor
her son's life. She put pen to paper
and the bard, with all his accolades, said
her letter became his most prized possession.

On the sixth day God looked upon
his creation and pronounced it very good—
the way the poet discovered wildflowers,
the way his daughter ate peach parfait.

When Cain killed Abel it started *The Troubles*.
Eve never received a poem honoring
her ice-cream son—her heart was given
the hard task of loving the assassin,
no poet to remind her that
in the beginning were the words,
"Let there be light," so that
(after the blood is washed from the streets
which house the flower shops for widows
and twenty-one flavors for children)
evening will pass and morning will come
and the new day will announce
that it's up to us, by proxy, to say
what is good to mark the sixth day.

|||

Where there is ruin, there is hope for a treasure.

—JALAL AL-DIN RUMI

THE LONGEST DREAM IN THE WORLD

Alexei Navalny has this dream
for peace and harmony and justice—
a deep knowing about
the natural order of things,
despite "survival of the fittest,"
despite military conquerors preaching
"to the victor belong the spoils,"
despite disagreeable clergy
recruiting the next army
of chosen ones to proselytize
in God's preferred language.

"Might makes right"
is so much of human history,
"Might for right"
still languishing in second place;
but the great teachers of humanity
were oceans of love.
Kings, presidents, emperors—
rivers dependent on snowmelt.

The longest dream hasn't died.
Dreams are not subject to death
like ideologies, one stacked
upon the archeology of the other—
a palace of ruins.

Only an image or a likeness
of a dream can inspire
or expire within the walls

of a temple. The dream,
like the wind, is the breath
of the world.

EASTER, PASSOVER, RAMADAN

(three songs, three feasts, three fastings)

What keeps us from saying *Amen* in one voice?
The anvil, hammer, and stirrup bones of the inner
ear are trustworthy steeds, but servants
to the familiar, bridled and saddled for journey,
yet prefer the known voices of loved ones,
the familiar bells of the village, local sermons
of birds in the garden that comfort illness.

The sound of your own destiny insists, in whispers,
that you break through the din of the ordinary,
like a recruiting sergeant saying, "make your mark,"
like the song of a mate saying, "come hither,"
or the voice of a messiah that shatters
the rhythm of mediocrity.
                            Drop the familiar
tune, the voices of comfort: the coffeepot,
the key in the door, any echo of engines
that propels you. Follow the rapture
of your destiny—the principle that allows
what is possible to happen—a babe in a manger,
a babe in the bulrushes, the illiterate scribe
of the messenger angel who becomes a fisher
of men and women.

                            The pharaoh's daughter heard
a cry and saved us with an answer to the question,
"Does God hear pain?"
                            Remove the sandals from your feet
because the place upon which you stand

is holy ground—resist that inner voice,
the *a cappella* song: "I'm not worthy,"
uttered with uncircumcised lips.
                                        Let
your life tell the story of an Exodus,
let the angel of death pass over
your blood-stained door, let your song
resurrect the hearts of others. Eat your meal
in haste because the pharaoh pursues you.
Get rid of the notion of leavened bread
because there is no time to let it rise.
Throw away your belongings and rush
with what you love to the train platform.
Take up your cloak and follow. Let
your voice join the communal prayer.
There must be lessons learned by the persecuted
if they are to have a future. The wise son
and the wicked son ask questions that can only
be answered by the feminine. Five million
women and children revise the Exodus story
as if Moses stays to fight when the sea parts,
as if Mohammed preaches without the trust
of Khadija, as if Adam could deal with the problem
of Cain and Abel without the hand of Eve,
as if God himself did not anticipate
with joy the coming of the Sabbath Bride.

Shalom. Salaam. Peace be with you.

PARTITION

Britain's 1947 partition of India
wiped out extended families,
turned rice paddies into killing fields.
Survivors looked for bodies of the missing.

Sikhs, Hindus, fled what is now called
Pakistan. Sudarshana Rani looks,
to this day, for her five-year-old brother
(now, seven decades later) in the market,
at the theater, in every crowd. She
and another brother were spared, sheltered
by a Muslim family of a classmate in Lahore.

I have watched people my entire life
kneel at shrines, light candles, and pray—
I have always found these acts beautiful,
yet parochial—religions march under
many flags, speak the familiar language
of scripture like birds using their only voice
to describe the miracle of morning light.

There is only one religion—the religion
that shelters the refugee, that comforts the terrified.

LAST PRAYER BEFORE WE DESTROY
THE PLANET

"No one will survive," Mel Brooks said
comically and prophetically—"It's all going
to go," says the environmentalist raised
in the coastal community. A poet friend of mine
is still waiting for her brother to return
in his aircraft that flew off and was never found.
She calls it "The Long Night of Flying,"
describing both his trip to the unknown
and her life of constant longing for a resolution,
a heart with a missing piece, what feels like
an empty chamber; yet no chamber is empty,
but a room for light or darkness or air, cosmic
radiation of some kind, infrared, microwaves,
something unseen, unknown.
                                                    You enter a mosque,
a church, an ashram, needing solitude,
the comfort of prayer, of meditation, wanting
to connect with another dimension, as if you are
a radio with a dial that can find the right frequency,
which was always there, which is everywhere
but frequently drowned by sounds of greed and fear
a hair's-width-away from the station of joy
and love.
                   We turn on the television and see
the Oklahoma tornado, the Louisiana hurricane,
the California firestorm, the deliberate bombing
of Aleppo or Kyiv and start to tune our minds,
search for a place of comfort like hiding under
a desk or storming into the recruiter's office
in anger, to be a part of some chapter

in history, to play a role. We pray for peace
on earth, "Inshallah," we say, "God willing."
We say, "Thy will be done on earth as it is
in heaven," often punishing evil like Michael
with Lucifer, the victor getting heaven,
the defeated, hell. Perhaps the Mother of God's
time has come at last, the intercessor,
the one who comforts the tormented—the one
meant to answer the cry of the first murderer:

"Am I my brother's keeper?"
The question the sister has no need to ask.

FIRE ESCAPES

(after Ocean Vuong's Night Sky with Exit Wounds *and
Dante's* Inferno*)*

There can be tenderness or violence in language,
laws written for obedience, pledges
of allegiance, recitation of scripture
reducing feeling to vain repetitions.

Language can turn hamburger to steak tartare,
servants to maître d' or sommelier,
a rosy-cheeked toddler to collateral damage,
the biggest mistake of your life, to friendly fire.
Desperate refugees become invaders.

Victims of a forced march were once given
comfort blankets contaminated with Smallpox.
Napalm is a blanket of miscalculations,
not the immolation of a Buddhist monk
who set himself on fire because words
can fail in protest or in prayer. Sometimes
the body is the only language left
to offer as sacrifice. "No greater love than this…"

it was said, that we lay down
our lives for another; that we give up
our last bowl of rice to a child with distended
belly and welcome our own hunger pangs
to shock us into awareness that there is only
one body, one mind, one heart, searching endlessly
along many trails that all lead
to the same threshold.

TRANSFIGURATION

I read another story of a whale
trapped in a fish net, how she struggled
for unknown hours, how her mouth
could barely open for food, how she
approached utter exhaustion when the trawler
came upon her. How the men
didn't hesitate, how they fell into
unanimous duty, spontaneous common purpose.

How miraculous that the human brain's
evolved enough to invent oxygen tanks,
wet suits, the curved knife blade,
sharp as a razor, which can cut through
rope. Intriguing how the whale brain
knows to assume a passive position, accept
the kindness of strangers—a foreign species
with instruments of questionable intent.
How advanced her intuition and
the bravery of ordinary men
to labor near tail and fins
so powerful one slap is fatal.

And when the last binding chords were loosed
the lead diver stared into her giant eye
and was moved to depths never experienced
in the cathedral even at Easter. And the crew,
at peace in overwhelming fatigue,
watched her circle four times
in what all recognized as gratitude.

They would later speak of their own
gratitude for the gift of that day;
each of them researching whales
with renewed interest, curious what
goes on within the world's largest brain.
A brain so large yet has no library
of historical information to draw upon,
no scripture to ponder, to comfort, to postulate,
to solve mysteries like random kindness.
We can be sure, for instance, that the whale,
whatever it knows, knows that its rescue
had nothing to do with the transfiguration of Christ,
the labor of Simon, the mercy of Veronica.
We can all agree on that.

HOLY LAND

(Basilique du Sacré-Coeur de Montmartre)

We went to mass at Sacré Coeur
but first checked into our hotel,
found a café and had a latte,
absorbed city life, observed two
young couples at another table
flaunting their sexuality,
one couple sparring with words and eyes,
the other soft touches of affection;
all four smoking, and youth their answer
to everything. Each table seemed
to display some previously lived
segment of my life and each table
adorned with a carafe of water for thirst,
containers of brown sugar and tiny spoons
that made me smile at my extravagance,
my familiarity with tablespoon and teaspoon,
every privilege of large measure.

We climbed the steep streets, the scores
and scores of pastel-colored steps
to the basilica; it's architects
investing the bulk of their lives in order to give
anyone up to the task a greater vision
of a city in splendor—the perfect antidote
to a compartmented life, the keys
everyone carries in their pockets for the locks
we turn even while greeting a neighbor.

A choir of nuns welcomed us with practiced
harmony that could spur jealousy

if their habits did not remind us of sacrifices
we have never considered. Sacré-Coeur

is a metaphor for modern life—
security officers strategically placed
because God's words have been
vulnerable to many interpretations.

After mass, after the consecration
of the bread and wine, the ingestion of
the Christ, we walked the streets of Montmartre,

the canopied restaurants, the clink of wine
glasses, the aroma of crepes and pommes frites;
stopped to watch an artist draw a portrait
of a little boy expected to sit still
long enough for his parents to have
a more permanent memory.

We took it all in: the grumpy maître d',
the charming waitress, the mussels, the escargot,
the abundance of bread on the table,
the nationalities talking in tongues
that drifted over the linen tablecloth
onto the square. I spotted a brother and sister
laughing, comparing ice cream cones,
tongues working to offset the heat of their hands.

On the way to Charles de Gaulle I saw a beggar
on the side of the road holding a sign that read
SYRIAN REFUGEE. He tried to approach us
at a traffic light and the cabbie locked the doors.
Maybe he was a fraud. Maybe he wanted

money for drugs. Maybe if I used
all my faculties of reason I could
make sense of God. Maybe if I went
to Mecca or Jerusalem, instead
of Paris, I could finally be saved.

STAINED GLASS

Why did we stain the glass
rather than create an ordinary window?
Why did the carpenter make pews
without comfort, without privilege, just
one handicapped section? Why did we
have to have a sacrificial altar,
a dinner table without chairs, a vestal
virgin the only one qualified
to handle the bread and the wine?
Why did we ring a bell at the *imitatio*
of the Last Supper? To wake the daydreamers,
those hung-over from late night revelry?
Why did we light candles in an already
lit room? Why was incense necessary?
To represent the one who got away
from the undertaker, resurrected
not from the grave, not from
the womb of the mother, but from the tomb?

Why *do* we stain glass, dim the outside
world just enough to make incense
visible? Smoke seeking a way out,
beyond the tinted frames held together
by what I was told, as a child, was
the world's heaviest metal; but later learn
plutonium, uranium were heavier.

In the center of Hiroshima,
450 meters from Ground Zero,
stood the Nagarekawa Church
with an inspiring steeple, windows

designed to beautify ordinary light,
a sanctuary designed to transform
ordinary language, ordinary thinking, to:
Father forgive them, for they know not
what they do. Every church is constructed
by a bricklayer, a carpenter, a stained-
glass artisan. *Greater works than these*
you shall do, it was once said—so
that hands taught to fly the Enola Gay
could turn a window to a rose.

THE SOUL'S JOURNEY

(on hearing of the death of George Herbert Walker Bush)

In 1914 there was a Christmas truce
in the trenches along the Western Front.
Against all logic and reasoning
it made sense to sing *Silent Night*.
In the midst of great suffering
souls occasionally speak to souls.

President Bush died last night;
as a Navy pilot he was shot down
over the Pacific and rescued by
an American submarine deployed
to save one life no matter how
impractical. You might say
that's an example of the Golden Rule.

There are separate bodies and many minds
but the soul sits upon common ground,
a common sea—innumerable waves,
one stillness at its depth; one amniotic life
experienced by all before birth into
an individual identity. Angels
are not a different species than ourselves,
angels just have never taken on a robe,
a uniform, a body's slow movement
which retards self-discovery temporarily.

An infant's head has a soft spot at birth,
the fontanel slowly closing to the vastness
above—adepts have called it the Crown Center.

"Find your center," my mentor used to say;
find your regal-ness, the crown we are all
meant to wear, the place of anointing,
the place that makes the ceasefire possible.

THE SHAKING QUAKERS

(after watching a Ken Burns documentary)

They were called the Shaking Quakers,
led by a religious zealot, a refugee
from England, Mother Ann Lee,
who had a vision of Jesus, started a community
of loving kindness and good works,
industry without idolatry or profit motive—
though their works were widely sold, valued:
clothing and furniture, horseshoes and honey.
They were carpenters and seamstresses,
physicians, farriers, farmers. Their goal:
to imitate the life of Christ. Though
celibacy led to their extinction, they
claimed it essential spiritual energy.

How they could work! Houses of wood,
granite, limestone built to perfection,
invention a way of life, from nails to brooms,
from garments to architecture—but always
worship, meeting, singing and dancing,
male and female circles rotating,
like planets creating their own gravity.

In New Lebanon, New York,
they held the first Universal Peace Conference.
Lincoln granted them Conscientious Objection
during the war but said he could use men
like them, making you wonder about his own
religious sensibilities; forced to be
Commander in Chief of men who would slaughter

one another—crusaders in holy war—
but after victory, preached "malice toward none."

At Pleasant Hill, Kentucky, the Shakers found
some local townspeople had been sneaking
to their farm after dark and stealing
vegetables. So they planted more.
Their leader said, "We plant some for ourselves,
some for the thieves, and some for the crows.
Thieves and crows have to eat too."

"DO YOU KNOW GOD?"

They asked me earnestly
as if part of political polling
that would determine
the winning candidate.
I knew intuitively
that they wanted me
to ask the same question.
Their body language
more like someone holding
a bag full of groceries,
than one small black book.

I wondered at the near biological
drive to save others who are already
well-fed, possess decent shelter.
If I followed my first instinct
to protect thirty precious minutes
of my own mortal existence,
to preserve my practical
and comfortable daily routine,
if I said that I had something
on the stove or pending
FaceTime with grandchildren
and closed the door on them,
it would tarnish my Sabbath
with dishonesty, mirror
the Biblical story:
no more room at the Inn.

They did not resemble
the Iranian Magi

looking for answers
but rather simple farmers
driving a hay wagon
to the unloading place,
laden with sustenance
for those with the proper gut
to digest new grass.
Consider the lilies of the field
they told me—consider
the stature of mustard seed.

They left a pamphlet
that did not help me know God
and they left with a smile
that seemed to suggest
no better-than-even odds of me
entering those Pearly Gates
but perhaps better-than-even
for them for their effort.

I returned to the kitchen,
opened the spice rack,
the tabernacle containing
the salt, the pepper,
the cumin, the thyme, the sage,
the mustard seeds
ground down to a powder
so fine, so digestible,
that I might know
a mustard tree.

FORGIVE

*(United Nations Day—anniversary of the UN Charter,
October 24, 1945)*

Forgive the story the other needs
to survive—their boasting of curious facts
you recognize as fiction—their adroit
mapping the dark side of the moon, when you
only remember the different phases of light.
Forgive even the assault on the dogma
you trusted to be the antidote to malice—
forgive because it is your only evidence
of a force capable of quelling the animal cries
of the body—the will to fast when offered the feast—
the negative capability of love's arsenal—
Cupid's arrow turned into the only
battering ram which can prevail against
the gates of Hell.

THE SHAPE OF YOUR OWN ABSENCE

The more generous you are the wider the ripples
produced by your simple dropping of stones.
You bring your child to the pond and collect
a few gifts ground down by the centuries
for human fingers to manage. You listen together
to birdsong and then begin the pedagogy
of difference rather than this ability to take
the weight of a small mortality and defy gravity.
The attempt to be invulnerable is to build
a house on sand. Vulnerability is the foundation
upon which we build, find shelter,
the nourishment needed to walk the hero's path.

Genius loci is finding oneself in the presence
of protective spirit, the whisper of waves
as you walk along the shore constantly looking
for a message in a bottle. Aladdin
could go to magical places, but needed
a magic carpet woven by the master,
could fulfill his greatest desires only
by asking the genius residing in the lamp.

Pick up the conch shell or any
orchestra pit large enough to fit
into the space of your hand, lift it
to your ear, listen until you recognize
the shape of your own small, essential, voice
in harmony with the breath of the ancient chorus.

LORD'S PRAYER

Our Father/Mother God
Who art in heaven which art the universe,
Hallowed be thy name, the first word,
The beginning bang of a drum
Whose echoes reverberate still.
Grant us Your patience and Divine Wisdom
For Thy kingdom will not come by expectation
But is spread upon the earth yet not seen
As Lucifer could not see it in heaven.
Continue each day Thy bounteous gifts
And forgive us our greed
As we forgive the greedy
And lead us to avoid temptation
With the image and likeness of Thy Will
For we know not what we do.
Grant us the mercy of Thine archangels
Whose voices cometh from within
Like the light visited upon the Virgin
So that we, too, can be delivered.
Amen.

GROUND ZERO

My wife's father was shot three times
by a Japanese Zero and lived to tell;
but he never did. My niece worked
on the 103rd floor of WTC II
and lost most of her co-workers.
She was coming up from the subway
when the second plane hit.
We've never discussed it.
She's never asked me a single question
about Afghanistan.

The Boeing 757s used on 9/11
were loaded with 87,000 lbs. of jet fuel,
for transcontinental flight,
as they are every single day without
hurting a soul. Fill a young man's
head with combustible ideas
and 3,000 people easily die.

We went to Ground Zero yesterday,
the national gravesite in NYC.
It is like no other grave—responders
are still coming, still climbing the stairs,
still tumbling down into those holes.

In the 9/11 museum
they have a short film by a graduate student
washing her firefighter father's shirt—

he came home covered in grime and sweat
and all manner of ashes-to-ashes and dust-
to-dust. She simply filmed her hands scrubbing
and scrubbing that officer's soiled white shirt
in a bathroom sink, trying to make it useable.

We walked out of the museum
to the two massive watery graves
that don't resemble any burial plot
you've seen; the water's constant movement,
its sound gifting the peace of walking a beach,
watching waves wash the shore, similar
to a daughter's hands kneading
and kneading a father's shirt, the way
we wish we could scrub our own souls,
draining every unnecessary act
into an ever-accepting well of kindness,
the open ground that reduces all pain
to zero.

IMMIGRATION

We are all immigrants;
immigrants from war,
immigrants from religion,
immigrants from dustbowls,
or mudslides, or tidal waves.
People have always fled
drought or flood.

Governments shift advantages too,
from Sunni to Shia,
from Jew to Christian,
from believer to atheist.
An infidel can have their head severed,
an antigovernment "hooligan" spend
a lifetime freezing in a Gulag.

We are all immigrants
from childhood illnesses or adult cancers
or bad marriages or fickle corporations.
Sometimes there is no time to emigrate
and you are absorbed by history—
Stalin's twenty million, Hitler's six,
Cambodia's two million plotted in killing fields,
Armenia's one million or Rwanda's near-
million slaughtered under the watchful
but impotent collective, wringing or
washing their hands; absorbed in their
own troubles, worried about how to
fill their own pantries for survival.

The potato famine killed over a million
men, women, and children in Ireland, and
caused another million to flee, my relatives
among them—all due to a fungus,
a naturally occurring fungus. The influenza
epidemic of 1918 killed
more people than World War I. There is
no inoculation against living
on planet earth, there is simply help
or the refusal of help.

Neil Armstrong said, "That's one small step
for man, one giant leap for mankind."
He was not referring to the lifeless dust
at his feet—but to the vision
over his shoulder, the black sea he had
crossed without capsizing, without sinking;
just another immigrant setting shore
hoping to have found, at long last,
the land of unity.

I CAN'T SEEM TO MEDITATE ANY LONGER

I went to the mountains of Afghanistan
but never made it out of the foothills
of the Himalayas, never met a rishi,
let alone sit with one in meditation.

I never learned to break down the wall
of "I am." My prayers built a bulwark
that said I am down here in the muck
while you sit majestically in heaven.

The problem of suffering in the world
frequently keeps me from joy—but then
I hear music, someone asks me to dance,
a dispensation that dares one to die

before death, prance on your own grave
before it is occupied. Laugh, because
that is the one sound you can still believe
is an answer to your prayers.

THE ARTIST WILL SAVE US

When the brutal society has its way
with us, when it unlocks every dark
corner of our soul, turning neighbor
against neighbor, brother against sister,
when it is done seducing every kind
tendency out of us, pointing out
its lack of utility, when the hard
trades are glorified and the soft hands
of the money men grip the calloused hands
of the worker at the political rally
because they own them, when the arts
and history itself are denigrated,
 re-written, so that the journalist
and the poet are characterized as elitist,
dangerous, enemies of the state—
the artist will save us.

The artist will write the song of the nation
that opens the tear ducts of the sinner.
The story will be told by some filmmaker
or composer, and will even win awards
because the collective conscience needs
the unburdening of confession, knows:
without truth you drown in your own sewage.

Artists will suffer small wages, mostly
in obscurity, with a faith resembling
laborers who build the levee for an uncertain
eventuality; working against time,

hoping their page in the Greater Book is written,
gets recorded, while there is still belief
in a power willing to grant absolution.

ACKNOWLEDGMENTS

River Heron Review: "Naming Fireflies," "Among the Blessed," White Gloves"

U.S. 1 Worksheets: "Postmortem House Cleaning" (nominated for a Pushcart Prize), "The Sixth Day"

Schuylkill Valley Journal: "The Real Reason I Call Her My Better Half"

Moonstone Press: " Stained Glass," "The Space Beyond Repair," "The Laureate's Love Poems"

Carry Us to the Next Well (Kelsay Books): "I Can't Seem To Meditate Any Longer,"

Poetry For Change: "Immigration"

Bucks County Herald: "The Shape of Your Own Absence"

War, Literature & the Arts: "Bucha"

In gratitude for Terry Culleton, Bill Wunder, and Luray Gross who helped me with this manuscript in so many ways—their guidance and inspiration have been a gift to me; their poetry a gift to so many.

Many thanks to my editor and publisher, Ellen Foos, and to the family at Ragged Sky Press.

And to my wife, Barbara, your unending belief and support of my work and your unconditional love keep me afloat. Your work for social justice is a daily inspiration.

ABOUT THE AUTHOR

Steve Nolan did his undergraduate work at the University of Miami in English and Psychology and his Masters at Barry University, in clinical social work, also in Miami, Florida. He is a Licensed Clinical Social Worker who spent twenty-five years as a therapist and thirty years in the military ending his career as the Chief of Combat Stress for Paktika Province in Afghanistan. He ran a PTSD clinic for the VA for five years before moving to Newtown in 2015.

His work has been published in: *River Heron Review, War, Literature & the Arts, Passages North, U.S. 1 Worksheets, The Florida Review, , Gypsy (Amnesty International Edition), Schuylkill Valley Journal* and others. His poems were featured on Morning Edition, National Public Radio, 24 September, 2007, upon his return from Afghanistan, in a story called, "Mother, Son Share War Experiences."

He is the author of *Go Deep, Base Camp,* and *American Carnage: An Officer's Duty to Warn*. His work reflects his commitment to social justice.